The Dialectic of Spirit - Vol 1

The Dialectic of Spirit - Vol 1

Anurag Anurag

Contents

1

The Dialectic of Being and Nothingness

In the beginning, there is a simple notion—Being. It is the most abstract, indeterminate idea. Being, in its purest form, is devoid of any characteristics, distinctions, or qualifications. It just *is*. However, in its abstraction, pure Being reveals a profound paradox: by possessing no characteristics, it is indistinguishable from its opposite—Nothingness.

Nothingness, like Being, is a concept of absolute abstraction. It too is pure indeterminacy, the absence of all qualities. In this void, nothing is defined, nothing exists. But here arises the crucial insight of dialectics: Being and Nothingness are not static opposites. Rather, they are interdependent and inseparable. The concept of pure Being dissolves into Nothingness, just as Nothingness inevitably transforms into Being. They do not stand alone but are in constant flux, giving rise to Becoming.

The relationship between Being and Nothingness embodies the core principle of dialectics. Neither state can exist without the other. Being, when conceived in its purest form, lacks any specific determination and thus collapses into the emptiness of Nothingness. Conversely, pure Nothingness, when recognized, already implies the negation of itself, and thus it transitions into Being. This movement between Being and Nothingness reveals the dynamic nature of reality.

Hegel saw this movement as the foundation of all existence. For him, this process was not static or linear but an eternal cycle of transformation. In the interplay of Being and Nothingness, we find the origin of Becoming—the process by which everything in the universe emerges and evolves. Becoming is the synthesis of the dialectical tension between Being and Nothingness. It is the truth of both concepts and the process that defines the world as we experience it.

In the dialectical unfolding, Becoming represents the unity of opposites. It is the synthesis of Being and Nothingness, capturing the essence of change, movement, and transformation. Becoming reflects the reality that nothing in existence is fixed or static; everything is in a constant state of flux, always moving from one state to another.

Becoming is a process of coming into being and ceasing to be. Every object, every idea, every moment is caught within this dynamic tension. When we speak of something "becoming," we acknowledge both its presence and its transitory nature. To become is to both exist and not exist simultaneously, to live in the threshold between appearance and disappearance.

For Hegel, the notion of Becoming carries profound philosophical implications. It suggests that the essence of reality is change, development, and transformation. Nothing is ever fully realized in a single, static state. Rather, everything is always in the process of unfolding, moving toward greater complexity, greater self-awareness, and greater unity.

The dialectical process between Being and Nothingness is not merely a philosophical exercise; it is the driving force of reality itself. Hegel's dialectic shows us that truth is not found in isolated, fixed categories but in the ongoing movement and interaction of opposites. It is through contradiction and resolution that knowledge advances, that existence evolves, and that freedom is realized. This method will underpin our exploration of consciousness, freedom, and the nature of reality.

Becoming is the heart of all existence. In this movement, we come to understand that every moment in time, every phenomenon in nature, every action and thought is a product of this interplay between opposites. Nothing can be fully grasped in isolation; it is only in relation to its opposite that its true essence is revealed. Being gives way to Nothingness, and from that Nothingness, Being emerges again, enriched by the process. In this way, Becoming is not a final state but a constant progression, an unfolding reality that never ceases.

This dialectical process is not limited to the realm of abstract thought. It is visible in the natural world, in the cycles of life and death, growth and decay, creation and destruction. We see it in the rise and fall of civilizations, in the ebb and flow of human history. Everywhere, there is Becoming—a continuous development, a movement from one state of existence to another.

To fully grasp the nature of Becoming, we must recognize that it is not merely a transition between two fixed points. Instead, it is the very process that defines and shapes reality. In the dialectic of Being and Nothingness, Becoming is not just a passage; it is the realization of both Being and Nothingness in their most dynamic form. It is the movement that brings about new realities, new possibilities, and new levels of consciousness.

Becoming is, therefore, the engine of all development. In philosophy, as in life, we see that progress does not come from stasis or rigid adherence to fixed categories. Rather, it emerges from the tension and conflict between opposites. In this way, contradiction is not something to be avoided or resolved prematurely; it is the very source of growth. Through contradiction, thought advances, and through contradiction, reality unfolds.

This understanding of Becoming as the driving force of existence leads us to a crucial insight about the nature of knowledge and truth. In Hegel's view, truth is not static or immutable. It is not a set of unchanging principles that we simply discover and apply. Rather, truth itself is a process—something that evolves over time, through the dialectical movement of ideas. Just as Being and Nothingness give rise to Becoming, so too do opposing concepts and ideas give rise to new forms of understanding.

In this sense, truth is always dynamic, always in motion. It is not something that can be grasped once and for all, but something that must be continually sought, continually redefined. The moment we believe we have arrived at a final, absolute truth, we are merely at the threshold of a new dialectical process. The synthesis we have achieved will soon reveal itself to be the starting point for another cycle of development, another unfolding of reality.

This process is not limited to individual understanding but extends to the collective development of humanity. Just as individuals undergo a process of becoming—growing, learning, evolving—so too does the human species. Our collective consciousness, our societal structures, our cultural achievements are all products of this dialectical unfolding. History itself is a record of Becoming, the story of humanity's progression from simple beginnings to increasingly complex forms of social, political, and spiritual organization.

In recognizing the dialectic of Being and Nothingness, we begin to see that history is not a random series of events but a rational process, driven by the unfolding of Spirit. Spirit, in Hegel's philosophy, is the collective consciousness of humanity, the force that drives us toward freedom, self-awareness, and unity. It is through the process of Becoming that Spirit realizes itself in the world, moving from mere potentiality to actuality.

2

Subject and Object: Consciousness Evolving

The development of consciousness is the story of the relationship between **Subject** and **Object**—a relationship that lies at the heart of human experience. At its most fundamental level, this relationship is the very structure through which we engage with the world. The subject, as the perceiving and experiencing self, is constantly interacting with the object, the external world that it perceives. But this interaction is not static; it evolves. The subject does not remain a passive observer, and the object is not a mere static entity. Together, they shape and reshape each other in a dynamic process of development.

The dialectical evolution of consciousness unfolds through this interaction. The subject is not merely confronted by the object; it seeks to understand it, to internalize it, to bring the external world into its own realm of thought. At the same time, the object is not simply imposed upon the subject. It resists, challenges, and defines the subject in return. Through this tension, consciousness evolves.

In the earliest stages of consciousness, the subject experiences the object as something entirely separate, alien, and external. The object exists as a brute fact, something that stands in stark contrast to the subject's internal world of thought and feeling. In this stage, the subject is aware of its own separateness but has not yet come to fully understand its relationship with the object. This is the state of **immediate consciousness**, where the world is encountered as "other," and the subject feels a sense of detachment from it.

But this separation cannot last. The subject, driven by its own nature, seeks to comprehend the object, to bridge the gap between itself and the external world. This leads to a higher stage of consciousness—**perceptual consciousness**—where the subject begins to organize and categorize the objects of experience. At this point, consciousness is no longer simply observing the world; it is actively engaging with it, attempting to make sense of the multitude of sensations, experiences, and phenomena that it encounters.

Through perception, the subject imposes order on the chaos of the external world. Objects are no longer seen as isolated entities; they become part of a larger system of relations, connected by space, time, and causality. Yet, even in this stage, the subject still experiences a fundamental duality between itself and the object. The object is understood and categorized, but it remains outside the subject, something to be known and classified.

As consciousness continues to evolve, it moves beyond mere perception to **self-consciousness**. At this stage, the subject begins to recognize that the object is not wholly other, that the external world is, in fact, deeply connected to the subject's own being. In perceiving the object, the subject comes to see itself. The act of perception reveals not just the world, but the subject's place within it. This moment of self-awareness marks a critical turning point in the evolution of consciousness, for it is here that the subject begins to understand that it is not simply an observer of the world but an active participant in it.

Self-consciousness introduces a new dynamic into the relationship between subject and object. The subject now realizes that it is not just defined by the object, but also defines the object in return. The external world is no longer something that exists independently of the subject's perception of it. Instead, the subject begins to see that its own thoughts, desires, and actions play a crucial role in shaping the object. The world, in a sense, becomes a reflection of the subject's own inner life.

But with this newfound awareness comes conflict. The subject, in recognizing its power over the object, also becomes aware of the limits of that power. The external world resists total assimilation into the subject's consciousness. There are aspects of the object that remain stubbornly independent, that cannot be fully grasped or controlled. This tension between the subject's desire for mastery and the object's resistance is what drives the further evolution of consciousness.

This tension reaches its highest point in the famous **master-slave dialectic**, a metaphor for the struggle between consciousnesses that occurs when self-conscious subjects encounter one another. In this dialectic, one subject attempts to assert its dominance over the other, to impose its will on the object (the other subject). Yet, through this struggle, both subjects come to realize that true self-consciousness cannot be achieved through domination. The master, in attempting to subjugate the other, finds that it is only through mutual recognition—through a relationship of equality—that self-consciousness can truly evolve.

At this stage, consciousness has moved beyond the simple binary of subject and object. It has come to understand that subject and object are not fixed entities, but are continually shaped and reshaped by their interaction. The subject cannot exist in isolation from the object, nor can the object be fully understood without reference to the subject. The two are deeply interconnected, each influencing the evolution of the other.

As consciousness evolves further, it begins to see that the distinction between subject and object is ultimately illusory. The two are aspects of the same reality, different expressions of a single, unified whole. This realization leads to the final stage in the evolution of consciousness—**absolute knowledge**. In absolute knowledge, the subject no longer sees itself as separate from the object. Instead, it recognizes that the entire process of subject-object interaction has been a movement toward unity. The world, in all its complexity, is understood as an expression of the subject's own self-realization, and the subject, in turn, sees itself as a part of the world's unfolding.

This process of evolving consciousness is not just an abstract philosophical idea; it is the story of human history itself. As individuals and as societies, we are constantly engaged in the dialectical process of subject and object, shaping and being by the world around us. Through this process, we come to greater self-awareness, greater understanding, and ultimately, greater freedom.

The evolution of consciousness is a journey through which the subject, initially separated from the object, comes to understand its profound connection to the external world. This relationship, characterized by tension and resolution, is the engine that drives consciousness toward higher levels of self-awareness and knowledge. From the simple immediacy of perceiving the world as "other" to the ultimate realization of unity in absolute knowledge, this process reflects not only an individual's intellectual growth but the development of humanity's collective consciousness.

The subject's interaction with the object is not a one-way encounter. It is a dynamic exchange, where both the subject and the object are continuously shaped by each other. This dialectical movement—from perception to self-consciousness and beyond—is a reflection of the evolving complexity of thought, society, and history. The boundary between subject and object gradually dissolves, revealing the fundamental truth that consciousness is an active process of becoming, rather than a static state.

As we move forward, this foundational concept of subject-object interaction will guide our deeper exploration into the development of freedom, reason, and spirit. The evolving consciousness is not just a philosophical abstraction, but a lived reality, one that unfolds both in individual lives and in the collective progress of human civilization. Through this lens, we will continue to uncover the dialectical movement that shapes not only thought but existence itself.

3

Self-Consciousness and Struggle for Recognition

The emergence of self-consciousness marks a pivotal moment in the evolution of consciousness. Unlike the earlier stages where the subject perceives itself as distinct from the object, self-consciousness arises when the subject turns inward and becomes aware of itself. This self-awareness, however, is not an isolated phenomenon; it emerges through interaction with others and the external world. At its core, self-consciousness is relational—it exists only through recognition.

To be self-conscious is to see oneself as both a subject and an object. The subject realizes that it is not only perceiving the world but is also being perceived. This dual awareness introduces a profound complexity to the subject's understanding of itself. It is no longer sufficient to simply exist; the subject now seeks validation, acknowledgment, and recognition from others to affirm its existence as a self.

The **struggle for recognition** begins with this need for validation. For self-consciousness to fully develop, the subject must engage with another self-conscious being. This encounter is not passive or harmonious; it is often marked by conflict and struggle. Each self-consciousness demands recognition from the other, yet both resist being reduced to an object for the other's validation. This tension creates a dynamic interplay that shapes the development of both parties.

In Hegelian philosophy, this struggle for recognition is famously illustrated by the **master-slave dialectic**. In this allegory, two self-conscious individuals encounter one another, each seeking to assert their independence. This leads to a struggle in which one emerges as the master and the other as the slave. The master achieves recognition by asserting dominance, but this recognition is ultimately hollow. The slave, in submitting, provides the recognition the master desires, but the master realizes that recognition from a subordinate being lacks the authenticity they crave.

Paradoxically, it is the slave, through labor and engagement with the material world, who gains a deeper understanding of reality and selfhood. By transforming the external world through work, the slave discovers their creative power and, in doing so, begins to assert their independence. The master, detached from the process of creation, becomes dependent on the slave for recognition. This inversion of roles demonstrates that true self-consciousness cannot be achieved through domination. Instead, it requires mutual recognition—a relationship of equality where each self-consciousness affirms the other as an independent and free being.

The struggle for recognition extends beyond the individual. It is reflected in the dynamics of societies, cultures, and histories. Human history can be understood as a series of struggles for recognition—whether through revolutions, movements for equality, or the fight for civil rights. These struggles are driven by the desire for freedom and the need to be acknowledged as autonomous individuals within a collective.

Recognition is not merely an affirmation of existence; it is the foundation of freedom. To be recognized is to have one's dignity, autonomy, and worth affirmed. Without recognition, self-consciousness remains incomplete, trapped in a cycle of insecurity and alienation. Mutual recognition, on the other hand, creates the conditions for genuine freedom, where individuals can coexist as equals, each affirming the other's independence while maintaining their own.

The struggle for recognition also sheds light on the nature of relationships and community. In every interaction, there is a negotiation of identity and acknowledgment. Whether in personal relationships, societal structures, or global interactions, the need for recognition shapes the way individuals and groups relate to one another. It is through this process that communities are formed, conflicts are resolved, and societies evolve.

The struggle for recognition does not merely unfold on an individual level but also manifests in collective dimensions. Nations, cultures, and ideologies engage in their own forms of recognition battles, each seeking validation of their identity, autonomy, and values. These larger struggles are not separate from the individual experience; rather, they reflect the aggregated desires of countless individuals seeking acknowledgment within their collective identities.

At the heart of this dynamic is the paradox of recognition. On the one hand, recognition is a deeply personal and individual experience—each person seeks to affirm their own unique identity. On the other hand, recognition is inherently relational and interdependent. No one can fully recognize themselves without the acknowledgment of another. This interdependence binds individuals and communities together, but it also creates friction, as each seeks recognition on their own terms.

This paradox can lead to alienation when recognition is denied. Denial of recognition is a powerful force—it diminishes the individual or group's sense of worth and autonomy. It creates a feeling of invisibility, of being reduced to an object rather than affirmed as a subject. This alienation often becomes the catalyst for resistance, rebellion, and movements for liberation. The oppressed, like the slave in the master-slave dialectic, find ways to assert their agency and demand recognition, challenging the systems that deny their humanity.

The historical trajectory of recognition reveals that this struggle is both transformative and progressive. Each stage of recognition, though fraught with conflict, paves the way for more inclusive and universal forms of acknowledgment. The movements for equality, civil rights, and human dignity reflect humanity's ongoing journey toward mutual recognition. These struggles, while rooted in the past, continue to shape the present and the future, as new forms of exclusion and denial arise, requiring new efforts for acknowledgment.

Recognition also plays a critical role in the development of institutions and ethical life. Laws, governments, and social norms are, in essence, frameworks for mutual recognition. They codify the rights and responsibilities of individuals and groups, creating the conditions for coexistence and cooperation. However, these frameworks are not static; they evolve as society's understanding of recognition deepens. What was once seen as acceptable or sufficient recognition may later be revealed as inadequate, prompting new struggles and reforms.

In personal relationships, the struggle for recognition is equally significant. Love, friendship, and familial bonds are built on the mutual acknowledgment of each other's individuality and autonomy. Without recognition, these relationships wither, leaving behind feelings of neglect or domination. True recognition in relationships requires vulnerability, openness, and the willingness to see the other not as an extension of oneself but as an independent, valuable being.

As consciousness evolves, so too does the nature of recognition. At its highest stage, recognition transcends the simple acknowledgment of individuality and moves toward the realization of universal interconnectedness. In this stage, the subject sees not only itself in the other but recognizes the shared essence that unites all beings. This universal recognition forms the basis of ethical life and spiritual awareness, where the boundaries between self and other dissolve into a higher unity.

The ultimate goal of the struggle for recognition is freedom. Freedom, in this sense, is not merely the absence of constraint but the presence of mutual acknowledgment and affirmation. It is the ability to exist as oneself while affirming the existence of others. This freedom is achieved not through domination or submission but through the reciprocal process of giving and receiving recognition.

As we conclude this chapter, it is clear that self-consciousness and the struggle for recognition are not isolated phenomena but are deeply embedded in the fabric of existence. They drive the evolution of individuals, relationships, societies, and history itself. The process of recognition, though often fraught with conflict, is ultimately a creative force, shaping the world and bringing it closer to unity and freedom.

4

Master-Slave Dialectic: Conflict and Freedom

The master-slave dialectic is one of the most profound and enduring elements of Hegelian philosophy. It captures the essence of human relationships as a struggle for recognition, where freedom and self-consciousness emerge through conflict and mutual dependence. In this dialectic, Hegel explores the dynamics of domination and servitude, revealing that freedom is not a given but a process achieved through struggle, realization, and transformation.

At the heart of the dialectic lies a confrontation between two self-conscious individuals. Each seeks recognition as an autonomous being, demanding acknowledgment of their independence and worth. This encounter, however, is not peaceful; it is marked by a clash of wills. Each self-consciousness refuses to simply be an object for the other. Instead, they strive to assert themselves as the subject, reducing the other to an object of recognition. This leads to a life-and-death struggle, where each risks everything to affirm their autonomy.

In this struggle, one individual emerges as the **master** and the other as the **slave**. The master asserts dominance, compelling the slave to submit and provide the recognition they seek. The slave, in turn, surrenders their independence in the face of the master's authority. On the surface, this dynamic appears to favor the master, who enjoys power and recognition. However, as the dialectic unfolds, it becomes clear that the master-slave relationship is fraught with contradictions and reversals.

The master's recognition, while seemingly achieved, is fundamentally hollow. The master depends on the slave for acknowledgment, but the slave's recognition is not freely given—it is coerced. True recognition, as Hegel shows, must come from an equal, a being capable of affirming the master's autonomy from a place of freedom. Since the slave is dominated and subjugated, their recognition lacks the authenticity the master desires. The master, despite their apparent dominance, is trapped in a relationship of dependency.

Conversely, the slave, through their subjugation, begins a transformative journey toward self-realization. The slave, tasked with laboring and engaging with the material world, discovers their creative power. Through work, the slave shapes the external world, imprinting their will and imagination upon it. This process of labor fosters self-awareness, as the slave comes to see themselves reflected in the objects they create. While the master remains detached from the material world, the slave engages with it directly, gaining a deeper understanding of reality and their role within it.

This reversal of roles reveals a profound truth: freedom and self-consciousness cannot be achieved through domination or subjugation. The master's position, though seemingly superior, is inherently unstable. The slave, through labor and self-discovery, moves toward independence and self-realization. The dialectic shows that both master and slave are bound by their interdependence, and true freedom can only emerge when this relationship evolves into mutual recognition.

The master-slave dialectic is not merely a historical or social allegory; it is a universal metaphor for the human condition. It reflects the struggles inherent in relationships, where power dynamics often obscure the deeper need for mutual acknowledgment. In personal interactions, societal structures, and even global politics, the dynamics of domination and servitude play out, shaping the course of history.

Hegel's dialectic also provides a framework for understanding liberation and progress. The slave's journey toward freedom mirrors the struggles of oppressed individuals and groups throughout history. By engaging with the world, asserting their agency, and demanding recognition, the oppressed challenge the structures of domination and pave the way for a more equal and just society. This process, while fraught with conflict, is essential for the realization of freedom.

The dialectic further illuminates the nature of freedom itself. Freedom, as Hegel conceives it, is not the absence of constraint but the presence of mutual recognition. It is the ability to exist as an autonomous being while acknowledging and affirming the autonomy of others. This higher form of freedom is achieved not through domination but through a relationship of equality, where each recognizes the other as a free and independent self-consciousness.

As we reflect on the master-slave dialectic, it becomes clear that freedom and self-consciousness are not static states but dynamic processes. They are achieved through struggle, conflict, and transformation. The dialectic teaches us that true freedom requires the dissolution of power imbalances and the establishment of mutual recognition. It is a journey that transcends domination and servitude, leading to a higher unity where individuals and societies can flourish.

The master-slave dialectic, though rooted in a philosophical framework, resonates deeply with the human experience across time and cultures. It speaks to the dynamics of power, dependency, and the quest for freedom that have shaped personal relationships, societal structures, and historical transformations. By examining this dialectic more closely, we uncover insights not only into the nature of consciousness but also into the mechanisms of change and liberation.

One of the most profound aspects of the dialectic is its emphasis on **labor as a path to self-realization.** The slave, through their engagement with the material world, gains an awareness of their capacity to shape and transform reality. This labor is not merely a means of survival but a creative act, a process through which the slave asserts their presence and agency in the world. By working on the object, the slave externalizes their inner will, leaving an imprint on the external world and, in doing so, begins to recognize themselves as an active force in shaping reality.

This realization is transformative. It breaks the illusion of the master's absolute power and reveals the potential for independence within the slave. The master, who remains detached from labor, is ultimately disconnected from the material world and the process of self-realization that labor provides. This irony—that the subordinate figure possesses the seeds of freedom—illustrates the instability of power dynamics based on domination.

The dialectic also highlights the inherent instability of relationships built on inequality. The master's reliance on the slave for recognition creates a paradoxical dependency. While the master appears to wield power, their sense of self is tied to the subordinate figure's acknowledgment. This dependency undermines the master's autonomy, revealing that true independence cannot be achieved through domination. Similarly, the slave's initial position of subjugation becomes the foundation for their journey toward self-awareness and freedom. This reversal of roles underscores the fluid and dynamic nature of power and consciousness.

These ideas are not confined to individual relationships but extend to broader social and political contexts. The master-slave dynamic is evident in the history of oppression and resistance, where dominant groups seek to maintain power by denying recognition to the oppressed. Yet, as Hegel shows, this domination is unsustainable. The oppressed, through their struggle and engagement with the world, gain a deeper understanding of their potential and demand recognition as equals. Movements for liberation, whether in the context of slavery, colonialism, or systemic inequality, reflect the dialectical process described by Hegel.

Hegel's insights into the master-slave dialectic also shed light on the nature of **freedom** in its truest form. Freedom is not merely the absence of external constraints but the ability to act and exist in a way that affirms both oneself and others. It is the realization of mutual recognition, where individuals and groups acknowledge each other's autonomy and dignity. This form of freedom is relational, requiring a transformation of the dynamics that perpetuate domination and inequality.

In modern contexts, the master-slave dialectic finds relevance in various spheres of life. In the workplace, for example, power dynamics often mirror the relationship between master and slave. Employers may seek to assert control over employees, yet it is the employees who, through their labor and creativity, drive the organization's success. Similarly, in politics and governance, the relationship between rulers and the ruled reflects the tension between domination and mutual recognition. Hegel's dialectic invites us to examine these dynamics critically and to seek pathways toward more equitable and affirming relationships.

The dialectic also resonates in personal relationships, where power imbalances can distort the mutual recognition that forms the basis of healthy connections. Whether in friendships, romantic partnerships, or family dynamics, the struggle for acknowledgment often mirrors the master-slave relationship. True intimacy and connection require moving beyond domination and submission, embracing equality and mutual affirmation.

As we conclude this exploration of the master-slave dialectic, we see that it is not merely a description of a historical or philosophical phenomenon but a profound lens through which to understand the human condition. It reveals that freedom, self-consciousness, and recognition are not static achievements but dynamic processes that unfold through conflict, engagement, and transformation.

This dialectic challenges us to rethink our assumptions about power, freedom, and relationships. It invites us to recognize the interdependence of individuals and to seek forms of interaction that transcend domination and lead to mutual growth. In this way, the master-slave dialectic serves as a blueprint for personal development, social progress, and the realization of a more just and equitable world.

The master-slave dialectic reveals a profound truth about the nature of human relationships, freedom, and self-consciousness: they are born out of conflict, struggle, and transformation. Through the confrontation of wills, the master and slave each come to realize that their existence is bound to the other, and neither can achieve true independence without mutual recognition. The dialectic teaches us that domination is inherently unstable and that genuine freedom is relational, achieved only when individuals and groups affirm one another's autonomy and dignity.

The journey of the slave from subjugation to self-awareness through labor illustrates the potential for transformation even in the face of oppression. It demonstrates that power and dependence are fluid, constantly shifting as individuals and societies engage with the material world and with one another. This dynamic is a microcosm of human history, where progress arises not from stasis but from the tensions and contradictions inherent in the struggle for recognition.

In our personal relationships, societal structures, and collective movements for justice, the master-slave dialectic continues to resonate. It reminds us that freedom is not simply the absence of control but the presence of equality, mutual acknowledgment, and shared humanity. By moving beyond domination and submission, we create the conditions for a more equitable and harmonious existence.

As we conclude this chapter, we see that the master-slave dialectic is not an endpoint but a gateway to deeper understanding. It serves as a foundation for exploring the broader themes of ethical life, reason, and Spirit in Hegelian philosophy. The struggle for recognition, though fraught with conflict, is ultimately a path to unity, freedom, and self-realization—a path that defines both individual lives and the collective journey of humanity.

5

The Evolution of Spirit

The concept of Spirit, or **Geist**, occupies a central place in Hegel's philosophy. Spirit represents the collective consciousness of humanity, the force that drives individuals and societies toward self-realization, freedom, and unity. It is not static; it evolves, progressing through a dialectical process from individuality to universality. This chapter explores how Spirit unfolds, moving beyond the confines of individual experience to embrace the universal, revealing the inter-connectedness of all existence.

The journey of Spirit begins with the **individual**, where consciousness is rooted in personal experience and subjective understanding. At this stage, the individual is primarily concerned with their immediate world—thoughts, desires, and relationships. Spirit exists in a fragmented state, as each person perceives themselves as isolated and distinct from others. This individuality, though essential, is limited. It does not yet recognize the deeper connections that bind individuals to one another and to the collective whole.

As Spirit evolves, it encounters the tension between individuality and the external world. This tension prompts a search for meaning beyond the self. Through interaction with others and engagement with society, the individual begins to see that their existence is not isolated but part of a larger network of relationships. This realization marks the transition from individuality to **community**. Spirit, at this stage, is no longer confined to the individual but begins to manifest in shared values, traditions, and social structures.

The community represents a significant step in the evolution of Spirit. It provides a framework for individuals to connect, collaborate, and find meaning beyond themselves. Yet, this connection is often imperfect. Communities can impose limitations on individuality, creating conflicts between personal freedom and collective norms. This tension drives the dialectical process forward, as Spirit seeks to reconcile these opposing forces.

The next stage in the evolution of Spirit is the emergence of **universal consciousness**. At this stage, Spirit transcends the boundaries of individual and communal identities, recognizing the shared essence of all humanity. This is the stage where Spirit moves from the particular to the universal, embracing the inter-connectedness of all beings. Here, Spirit understands that individuality and community are not opposites but expressions of a greater unity.

In universal consciousness, Spirit achieves a higher level of freedom and self-awareness. It no longer sees itself as confined to a single individual or group but as the collective expression of humanity's journey toward truth, freedom, and unity. This stage represents the realization of Spirit's potential, where the distinctions between self and other, individual and community, dissolve into a harmonious whole.

The evolution of Spirit is not merely a philosophical concept; it is reflected in human history and culture. Each stage of history represents a step in Spirit's journey, from the emergence of individuality in ancient societies to the development of universal principles in modern thought. Religions, philosophies, and social movements all reflect Spirit's quest for self-realization and freedom. They embody the tensions, conflicts, and resolutions that drive the dialectical process forward.

For Hegel, the ultimate realization of Spirit is found in **absolute knowledge**—a state where Spirit fully understands itself and its unity with the universe. This state is not static; it is the culmination of Spirit's dynamic journey through individuality, community, and universality. Absolute knowledge represents the synthesis of all contradictions, the point where Spirit transcends division and achieves complete self-awareness.

The implications of the evolution of Spirit are profound. It challenges us to see beyond our immediate, individual concerns and to recognize our place in the broader fabric of existence. It invites us to embrace the tensions and contradictions of life as part of a greater process of growth and transformation. And it reminds us that freedom and unity are not given but achieved through the ongoing dialectical movement of Spirit.

The evolution of Spirit from individuality to universality is not a smooth or linear process; it is marked by challenges, contradictions, and moments of crisis. Each stage of Spirit's development contains tensions that demand resolution, propelling it toward a higher synthesis. These moments of conflict are not failures but essential aspects of Spirit's journey, as growth emerges from the interplay of opposites.

One of the critical challenges Spirit faces in its evolution is the tension between personal freedom and collective responsibility. As individuals begin to recognize their role within a community, they often struggle with the constraints imposed by societal norms and institutions. Communities, while providing structure and meaning, can sometimes stifle creativity and individual expression. This tension prompts Spirit to question, adapt, and reform these structures, seeking a balance that honors both the individual and the collective.

Historical revolutions and cultural renaissances exemplify this dialectical movement. For example, the Enlightenment era marked a significant turning point in Spirit's evolution, as it championed individual reason and autonomy while laying the groundwork for universal principles such as human rights and equality. These developments reflected Spirit's attempt to reconcile the unique perspectives of individuals with the shared values of humanity.

Religion and philosophy play pivotal roles in Spirit's evolution. Religious traditions often embody Spirit's effort to bridge individuality and universality by connecting personal experiences to transcendent truths. For instance, the concept of divine unity in many spiritual systems symbolizes the realization that all beings are interconnected and part of a greater whole. Philosophy, on the other hand, provides a rational framework for understanding Spirit's journey, offering tools to analyze, critique, and synthesize its various stages.

Hegel's idea of Spirit as a historical force suggests that humanity's progress is not accidental but guided by a rational process. Each epoch represents a step in Spirit's unfolding, with its unique struggles and achievements contributing to the broader narrative of self-realization. Ancient civilizations, for example, emphasized the role of the community over the individual, while modern societies have increasingly focused on individual freedom. Both perspectives are integral to Spirit's journey, highlighting different aspects of its nature.

As Spirit moves closer to universality, it begins to transcend the divisions that separate individuals and communities. This transcendence does not erase differences but integrates them into a harmonious whole. Spirit recognizes that diversity is not a barrier to unity but a necessary condition for its realization. In this way, Spirit's evolution mirrors the complexity of life itself, where contradictions coexist and contribute to a richer understanding of existence.

The concept of universality in Spirit's evolution is not abstract or utopian; it has practical implications for how we live and interact with others. It challenges us to move beyond narrow perspectives and embrace a global consciousness that values empathy, cooperation, and mutual recognition. In a world marked by division and conflict, Spirit's journey offers a vision of hope, reminding us that unity is possible through the dialectical process of understanding and growth.

This vision is particularly relevant in the context of modern challenges such as globalization, climate change, and social inequality. These issues require a universal perspective that transcends individual and national interests. Spirit's evolution teaches us that progress comes from recognizing our interconnectedness and working together to address common goals. It reminds us that our individual actions are part of a larger collective effort to realize freedom, justice, and harmony.

As we reflect on the evolution of Spirit, we see that it is not just a philosophical concept but a call to action. It invites us to participate in the ongoing process of growth and transformation, to contribute to the unfolding of Spirit in our own lives and in the world around us. By embracing the dialectical movement from individuality to universality, we become active participants in Spirit's journey, shaping the future while learning from the past.

The evolution of Spirit from individuality to universality represents not only a philosophical idea but also a roadmap for humanity's collective progress. It teaches us that our differences—cultural, social, and personal—are not barriers but opportunities for growth. In recognizing the interconnectedness of all beings, Spirit evolves toward a greater understanding of itself and its purpose. This process is reflected in both personal experiences and the trajectory of civilizations.

On a personal level, the evolution of Spirit can be seen in the journey of self-discovery. Each individual begins life deeply rooted in individuality, focused on their personal desires, challenges, and achievements. Yet, as people engage with others and the broader world, they begin to encounter perspectives that challenge their own. This engagement, while sometimes uncomfortable, is essential for growth. By reconciling their individuality with the needs and values of others, individuals move closer to universality.

Take, for example, the development of empathy. Empathy is not an innate quality; it emerges through experience and reflection. When individuals confront the struggles and joys of others, they begin to transcend their own limited perspectives, recognizing the shared humanity that connects all people. In this sense, the evolution of Spirit is not a distant abstraction but a deeply personal process that unfolds through everyday interactions and choices.

Spirit's evolution is also evident in the development of social and political structures. Early societies often prioritized collective unity over individuality, creating rigid systems where personal freedom was subordinated to communal goals. As history progressed, revolutions, cultural movements, and philosophical ideas emerged to challenge these structures, advocating for the recognition of individual autonomy and rights. This tension between collective order and personal freedom drives the dialectical process of Spirit's unfolding.

However, these changes did not result in the abandonment of community. Instead, they led to a deeper understanding of the relationship between the individual and the collective. Societies began to recognize that individuality and universality are not mutually exclusive. Rather, they are complementary forces that must coexist for humanity to flourish. The push for human rights, equality, and global cooperation reflects Spirit's striving toward universality while honoring the uniqueness of each individual.

This tension and synthesis can also be seen in contemporary global challenges. Climate change, social inequality, and geopolitical conflicts all highlight the need for a universal perspective that transcends individual and national interests. These issues demonstrate that Spirit's evolution is ongoing, as humanity continues to grapple with the contradictions between self-interest and collective well-being. By addressing these challenges, humanity moves closer to the realization of Spirit's universal nature.

Art, religion, and philosophy have always been powerful expressions of Spirit's evolution. They reflect humanity's attempt to grapple with the fundamental questions of existence, meaning, and connection. Artistic expression reveals the shared emotions and experiences that unite individuals across cultures and time. Religion seeks to transcend the material world, pointing to a higher unity that encompasses all creation. Philosophy provides a framework for analyzing and understanding the journey of Spirit, offering insight into the patterns of growth, struggle, and reconciliation that define human life.

Hegel's conception of Spirit as a historical force reminds us that progress is not random but guided by a rational process. Each stage of history, while marked by conflict and upheaval, contributes to the greater unfolding of Spirit. This perspective invites us to see our own lives and struggles as part of a larger narrative. It challenges us to participate actively in Spirit's evolution by embracing change, seeking understanding, and working toward unity.

As Spirit evolves, it achieves greater levels of freedom and self-awareness. Freedom, in this context, is not merely the absence of constraints but the ability to act in harmony with oneself and others. It is the realization of one's individuality within the universal whole. This freedom is achieved through the dialectical process of reconciling opposites, integrating the unique and the shared, the personal and the collective.

The evolution of Spirit from individuality to universality is a profound journey of self-discovery, connection, and transcendence. It reflects humanity's collective progress, marked by tension, struggle, and eventual reconciliation. Spirit's path teaches us that individuality and universality are not opposing forces but interconnected dimensions of existence, each enriching the other. Through this dynamic process, Spirit reveals the unity underlying diversity and the potential for harmony amidst contradiction.

In this unfolding, we see that Spirit's journey is not a distant abstraction but an intimate and lived reality. It is present in the development of personal consciousness, the growth of communities, and the progress of societies throughout history. It calls us to engage actively with the world, to reconcile differences, and to strive toward understanding and unity.

As Spirit moves closer to universality, it offers humanity a vision of freedom and self-awareness rooted in mutual recognition and cooperation. It challenges us to rise above narrow, individualistic concerns and embrace the shared essence that connects all beings. By doing so, we participate in Spirit's ongoing evolution, shaping a future where individuality and universality coexist in harmony.

This chapter has traced the path of Spirit from its fragmented beginnings in individuality to its realization of unity in universality. This journey is not an endpoint but a continuous process, one that unfolds in every aspect of life and history. In the chapters to come, we will explore how Spirit's evolution manifests in ethical life, reason, and the unfolding of history, as it continues its timeless quest for truth, freedom, and self-realization.

6

The Conclusion of Volume 1: Foundations of Spirit

As we bring this volume to a close, we reflect on the profound journey of thought that has unfolded. From the interplay of Being and Nothingness, through the evolution of consciousness and the struggle for recognition, to the realization of Spirit's path from individuality to universality, we have traced the dynamic process that defines existence itself. These chapters have illuminated the dialectical nature of reality—a process marked by tension, contradiction, and resolution, driving both individual and collective growth.

The themes explored in this volume are not confined to abstract philosophy; they resonate deeply with the human condition. They reveal that freedom, self-awareness, and unity are not static achievements but ongoing endeavors. Every stage of development, whether of consciousness, Spirit, or society, is both a culmination of what came before and the foundation for what is yet to come. The dialectical process is a reminder that progress is born not from comfort but from the engagement with complexity and contradiction.

Volume 1 has laid the groundwork for understanding the fundamental principles of existence, thought, and self-realization. It challenges us to see beyond the surface of our experiences, to recognize the deeper patterns and processes that shape our lives and our world. This journey is far from over. In the volumes to come, we will delve further into the unfolding of Spirit in history, ethical life, and the ultimate reconciliation of thought and reality.

As we conclude, we are reminded that the journey of Spirit is not separate from our own. It invites us to participate actively in the dialectical process, to embrace the challenges and contradictions of life as opportunities for growth and transformation. In doing so, we contribute to the ongoing evolution of Spirit, shaping not only our own destinies but the collective future of humanity.

Volume 1 has been an exploration of beginnings—of the foundational concepts and movements that set the stage for what lies ahead. The path forward is one of discovery, as we continue to unravel the mysteries of existence, reason, and freedom. Let us move forward with curiosity, courage, and a commitment to understanding the unity that underpins all diversity.